POKÉMON COLLECTIBLES

Lisa Courtney

AMBERLEY

Acknowledgements

Thank you to my late grandparents for helping me grow the collection, and my mother for the same (plus for putting up with it all over the house!). Special shout-outs to Cornelios and Xemnas.

First published 2019

Amberley Publishing
The Hill, Stroud
Gloucestershire, GL5 4EP

www.amberley-books.com

Copyright © Lisa Courtney, 2019

The right of Lisa Courtney to be identified as the Author of this work has been asserted in accordance with the Copyrights, Designs and Patents Act 1988.

ISBN 978 1 4456 9730 7 (print)
ISBN 978 1 4456 9731 4 (ebook)

British Library Cataloguing in Publication Data.
A catalogue record for this book is available from the British Library.

Typeset in 10pt on 13pt Celeste.
Typesetting by Aura Technology and Software Services, India. Printed in the UK.

Contents

Introduction

Hasbro Nidorino combat figure.

Hello there! Welcome to the world of Pokémon collectibles. My name is Lisa. People call me the crazy Pokémon collector. This world is inhabited by collectibles featuring Pokémon! For some people, Pokémon collecting is a hobby. Others use it for profit. Myself, I study Pokémon collectibles as a profession.

Well, maybe not quite. But I think you know where it was headed.

As early as 1990, a game known only as *Capsule Monsters* had been pitched to Nintendo by a man named Satoshi Tajiri. The game was to feature monster battling by befriending the monsters, with over 200 of them to collect. Due to difficulties trademarking the name *Capsule Monsters*, the project was instead named *Capumon*. Later, the series became known by what would be the final name: *Pocket Monsters*.

On 27 February 1996, *Pocket Monsters Red* and *Pocket Monsters Green* burst onto the Japanese market. In the years that followed, millions of games with the Pocket Monsters name have sold, each continuing to pull new fans in and entice older fans to return. Pocket Monsters, known better overseas as simply Pokémon, spawned an extensive trading card game, multiple tournaments, dedicated stores, cafes, a theme park and so much more. Even today, Pokémon memorabilia of all types can be found around the world, always keeping collectors on their toes.

In this book, we'll be taking a look at the history of Pokémon collectibles and how the merchandise has evolved over time, as well as a few series that have stood the test of time. Of course, collecting is different for everyone – some choose to collect certain series of items. Some collect a certain type, such as figures or plushes. Some stick to items of specific Pokémon. Some collect everything they can (ahem, like me). As such, I'll try my best to pinpoint some of the most memorable and collectable of items wherever I can, whilst also covering as many different aspects of merchandise and aiming to document as many Pokémon as I can.

Since there are so many different routes to take out there in terms of availability, we'll be travelling down a simpler path. For the most part, this book will document the history of UK Pokémon collectibles, whilst also hopping over to Japan for further insight on some other beloved Pocket Monster collectibles. We won't set these rules in stone – a few items here and there might originate from other countries, such as the US.

Regardless of how you collect Pokémon, I hope you will find this book useful. For those looking to invoke feelings of nostalgia, I hope I am able to bring back only the fondest of memories for you. Without further ado, let's begin.

Chapter One
General

Before we take our journey across the regions, let's take a little look at some of the most collectible types of Pokémon merchandise, starting with some of the most recognisable. Many of these particular sets are very popular with collectors, and they span across multiple generations.

Whilst I won't go into too much depth with the Trading Card Game (solely because there are many more dedicated books out there), I'll gladly share a bit of history about the hugely popular Pokémon Trading Card Game.

With over 27 billion cards being sold worldwide, the Pokémon Trading Card Game (abbreviated by fans as PTCG, or even simply TCG when conversing with other fans) has been a gigantic success. The series was published by Media Factory in October 1996 until The Pokémon Company took over in Japan in 2013. In Europe, the TCG was handled by Wizards of the Coast until The Pokémon Company took over in 2003, around a decade before the same thing happened in Japan. There are over eighty different sets for fans to collect, and many other cards such as promo cards also keep collectors on their toes. Jumbo cards are another aspect that the die-hard collector will be interested in. Whilst not all series have a first edition print, those that do have potential to run into the thousands with the right card and condition (for instance, your unlimited base set Charizard probably

An assortment of Pokémon Trading Card items from over the years.

won't be worth thousands like those websites insist, because most have a habit of forgetting to show that first edition stamp in the example photograph). Keep an eye out for Shadowless base cards, too.

However, fans have discovered that there exists a card game believed to be even earlier than the TCG: a series that was released just one month earlier in Japan.

The Bandai Carddass set is a Japan exclusive series, reported as being released in September 1996 via vending machines at select stores. These images are based on the original Pokémon Red and Pokémon Green games that were out in Japan (and, in the case of Green, only in Japan). The series would eventually evolve into a series of cards based on the anime, but select cards are still sought after by certain collectors in all series, particularly the next series after this, which includes unique artwork.

It's no secret that the Japanese have their very own Pokémon stores, known as Pokémon Centers. Originally restricted to Tokyo and Osaka, the Pokémon Center chain has expanded greatly over the years, with some regions having access to multiple stores. Expansion has also seen the opening of two Pokémon Cafes attached to the Centers and even the opening of individual Pokémon Stores, including some airport

A selection of cards from the Bandai Carddass Set Parts 1 and 2.

shops. As one might expect, these stores are the ultimate dream for any collector, boasting a wide range of merchandise not available anywhere else. With the exception of the trading card game, the most sought-after merchandise tends to be Pokémon Center collectibles. Pokémon Centers have a diverse range of memorabilia, including but not limited to plushes, figures, bags, apparel, notebooks, keychains, food items, cards, stickers and so much more. Expect the unexpected as well – Pokémon Centers have been known to stock items that far exceed the bounds of regular collectibles. To put it simply, if a Pokémon version of any given object is available, the chances are it originated from a Pokémon Center.

Unlike many stores in the UK, the Pokémon Centers don't really keep merchandise on the shelves for too long. Instead of continuously restocking the same items for over a year (as fans have noticed some stores doing so over here in England), they frequently see items retiring, sometimes with a store span of only a month. When items do see a restock, they tend to feature either a noticeable design difference or a change in tags, so detecting a first edition release of their products is never too difficult. This is why merchandise from Pokémon Centers

Pokémon Center Tokyo during the tenth anniversary.

2005 and 2007 Pokémon Center artwork notebooks.

frequently leans on the more expensive side, and buying items immediately is arguably the best way forward when collecting items that are made here.

One of the many reasons that any fan should keep an eye on the Pokémon Center's website (even though you won't be able to order from them without a middleman) would have to be their beautiful designs. Tired of seeing that same Pikachu clipart slapped onto every item under the sun? Pokémon Centers have you covered. At any given point in time, the Pokémon Center will have a certain design available for purchase throughout the store. These designs are available on tins, pencil boards (known as shitajiki in Japan), clear files, sticker sheets, notepads, dice bags and more for the duration of the promotion. Best of all, more often than not they feature a large variety of Pokémon, including some that are rarely seen. Here are just a few more examples.

PokéDolls are one of the more famous brands of merchandise. These plush toys are based on the PokéDoll found in the original Red/Green/Blue games (hence the name), and are available in Pokémon Centers. However, they weren't always known by this name.

In 2001, Pokémon Centers in Japan released a brand of toys known as PlushPlush, a line of soft toys made to look like the PokéDolls in

Various examples of Pokémon Center artwork.

A selection of PokéDolls.

the game (a plush of a plush). These early versions are always sought after, no matter the character. Hang tags aside, the key difference between PlushPlush and PokéDolls is the materials used. A PlushPlush exclusively uses hard plastic eyes. All future iterations contain stitched eyes, and the material varies depending on the date produced. More recent PokéDolls use a velboa material. Whilst some PlushPlush and

PokéDolls see re-releases, some are less fortunate, such as Larvitar and Noctowl. Some have it even worse – Larvitar, in addition to never being re-released, never saw a release in America either, making the PlushPlush even more sought after. More recently, they have been rebranded as Pokémon Dolls, and differ significantly from their predecessors in their patterns. As an example, Squirtle features pure red eyes as opposed to the black eyes used in all previous iterations.

A fun bit of trivia: although these are Pokémon Center exclusive toys, the UK did, in fact, receive four PokéDolls back in 2003 – Pikachu, Torchic, Mudkip and Treecko. They were branded as 'soft toys' and distributed by Bandai, but are otherwise the same as their US counterparts.

Special release PokéDolls also exist, such as those seen here as well as the larger Pachirisu (limited release) and Charmander (contest prize) PokéDolls seen in the photo before this. They are usually limited time items or lottery items, and vary in size and material. These types of PokéDolls rarely ever see a release outside Japan, leaving even American collectors to seek out alternative means of collecting them. Shown here are three different Squirtle PokéDolls, with the centre Squirtle being the regular release PokéDoll.

Finally, PokéDoll merchandise also needs an honourable mention. Collectors of PokéDolls often find themselves mingling in with the PokéDoll merchandise collectors. There are many different items released containing illustrations of their PokéDoll counterparts,

From left to right: oversize, regular and mini Squirtle PokéDolls.

and locating these can prove more difficult than the actual PokéDoll sometimes, particularly with older merchandise and more obscure items such as sticker sheets. In fact, some illustrations used on these types of products can contain PokéDolls that never even existed in actual plush form, such as Regirock, Regice and Registeel.

Other plush toy lines that deserve an honourable mention: Pokémon Fit (a line which includes plushes from the first 251 Pokémon and all Unown forms) and Pokémon Canvas (a shorter series with small, pastel plush).

Tins are a favourite item for some people to collect and, whilst you may not have seen a great deal of Pokémon tins in the UK (barring the trading card game tins), Japan has been releasing Pokémon tins of all shapes and size for over two decades, many of them exclusive to Pokémon Centers. These often feature artwork that was used for a short time at the centers, as we mentioned earlier, making certain illustrations very sought-after. Sometimes, a figure or large can badge will be included on top of the tin, or an additional prize will be included inside.

Pokemon Kids figures are an extremely popular collectible. They are essentially small, hollow finger puppet figures made by Bandai.

An assortment of PokéDoll merchandise from a Pokémon Center.

A selection of Pokémon tins from the Pokémon Center.

Above left: Here are just a few more random tin examples hailing from the Kanto, Johto and Hoenn regions. Piffre tins, from left to right: Holiday, Piffre, Island (four angles).

Above right: Two Pokémon Center Christmas tins, 1998 and 2000.

Three Pokémon Center tins, from largest to smallest.

Since October 1996, over 300,000,000 of these inexpensive figures have been sold, making these lightweight collectibles one of the most successful lines in the Pokémon franchise. Best of all, there's at least one available for every Pokémon, making them the perfect collectable for people on a budget. In fact, they're so popular that Japan has even released a collector guide book for the tenth anniversary of the line.

The very first Pokémon Kids were released in Japan back in October 1996. These came packaged in a small box which included a piece of ramune candy, retailing for 100¥. In earlier series, there was also the possibility of pulling a rare clear variant from the box. Today, they are packaged in the exact same way, though clear variants are now available in box sets instead. DX Kids figures, although still hollow, are usually made with two pieces of plastic.

In the United Kingdom, we first saw Pokémon Kids in 1999, but very few even realised it at the time. They were available in similar boxes to the Japanese product, and even contained some candy just like the original. However, only ten were released: Ivysaur,

Pokémon Kids Perfect Collection Book and a selection of Pokémon Kids.

Deluxe collector's editions also exist, such as the one shown here, usually containing exclusive figures in the packs. Gallade DX Kid, Galvantula Kid and Pokémon Kids DX 97 set.

Cap Candy Collectible figure Pokémon Kids set.

Charmander, Squirtle, Pikachu, Wigglytuff, Golbat, Meowth, Geodude, Gengar and Snorlax. These figures featured minor colour differences to their Japanese counterparts, which would be a trend that would continue for select characters.

Starting from the Advanced Generation, the figures made a return to UK shelves and far more were produced. In some packages the centre featured a mystery Pokémon, which was often a clear variant. Others contained a DX Kids figure with some smaller Kids. These circular packages continued for several years until we received more rectangular casing towards the end of the Platinum era, scrapping the clear variant in the process. Heart Gold and Soul Silver continued with this type of casing, as did Black and White. Sadly, X and Y did not receive Kids figures in the UK, though they prevailed as always back in Japan.

Finally, in addition to clear figures, some select Pokémon also received shiny Kids figures, which are exclusive to Japan. These figures were typically given out in lotteries and are limited as a result, often reaching high prices on auction. Flocked Kids also exist, but only for a small amount of Pokémon, such as Charizard, Blastoise, Venusaur and Pikachu.

Pokémon Kids in the UK through the years.

Special Release Pokémon Kids – flocked, clear and regular Blastoise and regular, clear and shiny Ivysaur.

Monster Collection (also shortened to Moncolle) is one of the longest running lines in Pokémon's history. These hard plastic figures, usually measuring around 2–3 in., can be found in many locations. In Japan, they can be purchased individually for around 300¥ in stores around the country. Special editions, such as pearly, clear or shiny figures, can also be found for limited periods of time. Some figures are also available exclusively through other means, such as playsets, giveaways and more.

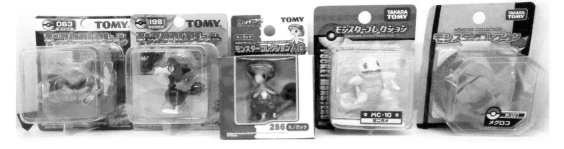

Japanese Monster Collection figures, from Kanto to Unova.

In the UK, these figures were distributed under Hasbro's license with various names given. They were available in two types of two-packs, two-packs with catcher PokéBall and badge, three-packs and special five-packs. The original human cast – Ash, Misty, Brock, Jessie and James – could also be purchased. These 5–6 in. figures came with one of their main Pokémon.

When the Advanced generation rose up, Bandai took over the license. Similar to the Hasbro released figures, they were typically packaged two to a box, and came packaged with cardboard discs of the respective

UK Battle figures and PokéBall Blaster 'Monster Collection' figures, plus James, Jessie, Misty, Ash and Brock Tomy figures. Shown here are a regular double pack, triple pack and the original trainer figures (not carded).

Monster Collection figures in the UK through the years.

Pokémon. After this, Tomy began to distribute the figures themselves, placing them in plastic cases. Variety was something that was present in this line when the figures were packaged in several different ways.

Zukan are a fan favourite item to collect, but they can be very pricey. For those not familiar with the Japanese version of Pokémon, Zukan is the original name for the Pokédex. So in English, these would be called Pokédex figures – if the companies cared enough to research the original name. To put it simply, Zukan figures are 1/40 scale figures of each Pokémon. These gashapon toys are arguably more fragile than Moncolle or Kids figures, but their attention to detail makes them highly sought after. Some larger figures, such as Wailord, were available only as lottery prizes in Japan, and some Zukan come with a more personalised base. In the UK, we also released some of these figures, under the name of Evolution Figures. For a while, they were identical to their Japanese counterparts, even retaining the Japanese names underneath their bases. Starting with the Regigigas Edition, the figures were made with a different type of plastic, which some collectors felt cheapened the overall appearance. The Zukan figures retired in the UK after Diamond and Pearl and have yet to return. In Japan, they are still being produced.

These larger figures were released in twin packs in the UK, but were tagged individually in Japan. Hasbro released several of these figures, including some more popular Pokémon, but Japan's Deluxe Collection figures held more variety and added several sought-after characters, such as the legendary bird trio, Vulpix and Dragonite. While the UK cut off the series after the craze died down, Japan continued to produce them and included characters such as the starters (it varied depending on whether they were final starters or beginning starters) and other various characters, such as Hondour.

Absol Zukan on base, plus an assortment of other Zukan figures.

Deluxe Collection figures (back to front, left to right: Houndour, Cyndaquil, Vulpix, Samurott, Articuno, Zapdos Moltres, Charizard, Eevee).

With over twenty different movies, merchandise for each is both limited and often sought after and, as can be expected due to the sands of time, earlier movie items can be troublesome to track down. In the UK, most movie merchandise is limited to the first movie, excluding the soundtracks, DVDs and occasional free trading cards. The watch and popcorn tub seen here are examples of the type of merchandise one might find in the UK.

Merchandise that is often considered desirable for this category includes the special edition Tomy Moncolle figures, limited release plush toys and the more unusual items, such as the Shaymin keychain and bracelet seen here. Items from earlier movies such as *Jirachi Wishmaker* and *Pokémon the Movie 2000: The Power of One* also find themselves in demand due to being less available at the time of release. Some items, such as the Deoxys and Rayquaza inflatables or drawing boards like the one featuring Absol and Jirachi, are seen as fun novelty items. With the right Pokémon, even an item that might not seem very appealing can command a high price. Other items that are often in demand are 'replica' items, such as the sketch book made for the release of *Pokémon Heroes* in Japan.

Many spin-off games receive merchandise in some form. Often these are smaller items such as a sticker sheet or a poster, though some spin-offs receive more merchandise, resulting in more collectors.

One such series is the Mystery Dungeon line, which boasts a surprising assortment of collectible goods. These games see you take the form of a Pokémon – the exact one is determined by your

Assortment of promotional movie items, Japan and the UK.

Kanon (Bianca's) Sketchbook. This book is a replica of the sketch book seen in the movie, and even includes a print of the Ash and Pikachu sketch handed to him at the end of the movie by either Bianca or Latias (since we never find out who actually kissed him there).

Pokémon Mystery Dungeon plush, stickers and game carry cases.

23

answers on a selection of questions presented on start-up and you can choose your own partner. Maybe it's due to how you form a close friendship with your partner Pokémon in-game, or it could be the idea of being a Pokémon yourself. Perhaps it could be because the games are genuinely fun to play. Whatever the reason, I find that Mystery Dungeon tends to have the most collectors where spin-offs are concerned. PokemonCenter.com released plush toys of Squirtle and Charmander featuring their signature bandanas for the release of the first two games, *Red Rescue Team* and *Blue Rescue Team*. Jakks Pacific issued a line of Mystery Dungeon plushes, where Pokémon also wore their bandanas. The game cartridge holders were made by BD&A, and were packaged with a screen cleaner and some stickers. Strangely, although the Red version features Charmander, as to be expected, they opted to use Pikachu instead of Squirtle for the Blue version.

Mystery Dungeon figures can be hard to track down nowadays and they are one of the more desirable items for collectors, particularly the series that included Kangaskhan's shop. The tiny Kangaskhan and Treecko here are also part of this collection. The strap figures were available in both the UK and Japan as gachapon prizes, and Turtwig is part of a diorama set and was also available to UK collectors.

There's still more merchandise out there of Mystery Dungeon, but we have more collectibles to get through!

The Metal Figure Collection is a common sight in Japanese auctions. However, this does not make them easier to collect, for a variety of reasons.

The figures are approximately 1 in. in size, and the method of obtaining them is through a blind box (as seen in the photo on page 25), which comes from gashapon machines. The most common sets are the Kanto sets, and many of these do not fetch very high prices unless you have a very popular character (such as Arcanine or Mew for

A selection of Mystery Dungeon figures.

Assorted Mystery Dungeon collectibles. The tin, sticker sheet and keychain strap originated from Japan's Pokémon Center, whereas the Shinx folder could be purchased in the US Pokémon Center. The badges were a free item in a magazine. The bookmark was a promotional item handed out at some stores to help promote the game, and the DVD was also a promotional item. To get it, you had to purchase one of the games from select stores and you would receive it for free.

Metal Collection 8 box plus a selection of Metal Collection figures.

example). The Johto Region metal figures are among the rarest to find, with certain popular figures such as the starters fetching high prices. Whilst it may seem like an easy task to collect an entire set, there's one more catch: each figure is available in five different metal finishes.

Gold, pewter, onyx, brass, copper and silver. In order to complete any set 100 per cent, you will need to obtain all the figures in the set plus the additional colours. If you're a more casual collector, of course, you can get away with just a single figure of each and call it a day. It's worth pointing out that the Kanto Pokémon can also be found in other colours, such as pink, green or blue, all with a metallic finish. In particular, collectors of a certain Pokémon will strive to obtain one of each individual colour, making a lot of these figures fairly valuable to the right buyer. As with most Pokémon collectibles, the individual Pokémon matters more than the set itself.

There's one other type of metal figure that collectors need to be aware of – Keshimon. Keshimon (*Keshi* being the Japanese word for 'eraser') are also blind packaged items which come in a rubber PokéBall of some type. These figures are much tinier, and are roughly half the size of a Metal Figure (so around 0.5 cm).

These figures are considerably rarer than Metal Figures, and have two colours available – Gold and Silver. The set would later evolve into KeshiPoke, which has a similar theme but replaces the metal figures with plastic ones instead.

Build-a-Bear is a company famous for allowing people to 'make a unique furry friend with clothing, accessories & more'. For the first time ever in 2016, a Build-a-Bear Pikachu was added to their line-up,

Gold, pewter, brass, copper and silver Gible figures.

Metal Collection Chansey and Keshimon figures. The Chansey in this photo is a Metal Figure, which should give you a rough idea of how much smaller these Pocket Monsters are.

whereupon the bundles proceeded to sell out so fast that many fans were left disappointed and unable to purchase a Pika of their own.

Eventually, Pikachu was restocked, and what followed were even more Build-a-Bear Pokémon toys. Although they could be purchased in stores, only one article of clothing and the plush itself were available, with each purchase including a Build-a-Bear promo card. Online, the plushes were sold as a bundle only, as part of a licensing agreement. The bundle usually consisted of the plush, a piece of clothing and an exclusive second piece of clothing or an exclusive accessory, the trading card and a voice box. Some other clothing and accessories also popped up, albeit silently. This can give you a good idea of how well some of these outfits can mix and match with each other, although some, such as Bulbasaur or Jigglypuff, can include nightmarish attempts at finding Build-a-Bear apparel that will actually fit them without looking strange.

The bulk of the Build-a-Bear range once again consists of primarily Kanto Pokémon, though a couple of other generations have also started to sneak in. At the time of writing, the collection consists of Pikachu, Eevee, Charmander, Squirtle, Bulbasaur, Jigglypuff, Snorlax, Vulpix, Alolan Vulpix, Meowth, Piplup, Psyduck and Snubbull, with the latter two being released for *Detective Pikachu*. The Build-a-Bear Pokémon that remain the most sought-after (and, at the time of writing, are out of stock) are Vulpix, Alolan Vulpix and Bulbasaur,

Above left: Build-a-Bear Pikachu.

Above right: Build-a-Bear Bulbasaur, Vulpix and Alolan Vulpix.

with or without the exclusive voice box inside. It's unknown if they will ever see another release in the future. Due to the production of these plush toys, it's recommended you buy them as soon as they come up for sale, otherwise you risk them going out of stock early.

One final observation about the Build-a-Bear plush would be their Eevee. Unlike the others currently in circulation, Eevee has what could be considered a 'first edition' printing. Initially, Eevee Build-a-Bears were printed with brown eyes. Shortly after this, all later editions were printed with jet black eyes. This is the only Build-a-Bear thus far to receive a significant design change. If you decide to get a Build-a-Bear of your own, go wild!

A collectible that has spanned most regions, these figural keyrings (see page 29) also come with a snap-open PokéBall. The series typically consists of around four characters, and a few series were also repackaged in a collector's box. A smaller line, Tag-Alongs, included a mini PokéBall and a mini figural keychain using the small mold as the normal keychains, only much smaller. This entire line includes a variety of Pokémon, mostly those considered to be more marketable (like the starter Pokémon for example, or the Pokémon featured in movies or shorts such as Buizel, Bonsly, Regigigas or Shaymin).

Pokémon Sliders by character are mostly hollow figures with a ball bearing at the bottom. They were one of the most well-known types of collectible back in the day and even saw a brief return during the Hoenn era. The advanced generation included Pikachu, Blastoise and Poliwhirl, which are ultimately re-releases of the original figures with an updated base to match the colour of the other Sliders in this series.

Build-a-Bear Eevee, original release (right) and later release (left). Please note that these are not the original outfits for Eevee. The Eevee on the right is sporting Jigglypuff's cape and signature microphone.

Series 12 and Series 17 keychain collector box sets.

Pokémon Sliders Arcade, original and Advanced Gen releases. Shown here are the Battle Arcade games, which came with four exclusive characters on the original release (Oddish, Rhyhorn and fan favourites Eevee and Charizard).

The original series had a total of twelve figures to collect (including the exclusives). The Hoenn release had twelve figures (including the Battle Arcade figures) in the set, though of those, only three were brand new – Mudkip, Treecko and Torchic, who can be seen later on. All others were re-released Sliders from the Kanto sets.

A series that never gained the popularity that it was supposed to, The Pokémon Trading Figure Game (often abbreviated to 'TFG' by fans) was a short-lived series introduced around 2006. The game involved a lot of spinning, collecting, and blind boxed figures.

The first series, 'Next Quest', contained forty-two figures to collect, each with a different rarity plus eight trading cards that could be used during play. Three box sets were produced: Riptide (containing Feraligatr, Murkrow, Pikachu and Brendan), Flamethrower (containing Charizard, Meowth, Treecko and Red) and Battle Starter (containing all figures from the previous two single player sets, plus an additional exclusive figure, the Referee). Whilst Riptide and Flamethrower were both widely available, collectors saw the Battle Starter set receive a more limited release, making the Referee a particularly rare figure overall.

'Next Quest' Battle Starter.

'Next Quest' Absol figures (left to right: First Edition, Pearl, Crystal).

Speaking of rarity, figures were available in unlimited and first edition forms, much like some trading cards. A first edition figure proudly displays a silver symbol on the side of the figure stand. Limited to rare figures only, a super-rare Pearl variant could also be found in boxes. Finally, although not seen in the UK, the US saw the release of a small number of Crystal figures.

Unfortunately, the series did not do as well as hoped, and the second set, 'Groundbreaker', was eventually cancelled after numerous delays. A small amount of the two starter sets, Skydive and Whirlwind, were released in some Walmart stores in the US, but the single figures never saw an official release. Despite this, the figures scheduled for both 'Groundbreaker' and an unnamed third set have been appearing in auctions online, though their authenticity is unknown.

Candy Catchers, or as they are better known in Japan, Pokémon de Catch, are a collection of candy dispensers not unlike Pez (which also exist in the world of Pokémon collectibles, by the way). These toys were released in Japan (and the initial set was also available in the

Assortment of Pokémon Candy Catchers.

USA) and produced by Bandai, but enough have been sold over the years that they pop up in UK sales posts from time to time as well. Packaging over the years has changed from a bubble pack to a box, though the products retain their original designs. Much like Pez, refill candy packets were also available.

The UK has had a rather rough time with Pokémon magazines. The very first magazine, known as *Pokémon Official Magazine*, was released in autumn 2004 as a quarterly magazine. This chunky magazine was in many ways like a Pokémon version of the *Official Nintendo Magazine*, packed with information about all aspects of the Pokémon scene. Sadly, the magazine was difficult for some fans to locate and did not sell as well as planned, and was cancelled after the second issue.

In April 2013, a new magazine was announced: *Pokémon: The Official Magazine*, released under the watchful eyes of Future Publishing. An advertisement showed the magazine as being bulky like the previous

Pokémon Official Magazine, *Pokémon* magazine and *Pokémon The Official Magazine* First issues.

magazine, and fans were thrilled. Upon release, the magazine received vocal criticism for being slim and not at all like the preview image had shown it to be. Further criticism from older fans was that, despite being aimed towards the same age group as *Pokémon Official Magazine*, the content was much more childish and lacking real substance. Additionally, those who pre-ordered a subscription received the regular magazine, whereas those who purchased it direct from stores received the issue shown here, with the additional free door hangers, punishing subscribers right off the bat. After many disgruntled fans cancelled their subscriptions, the magazine began to include an A4 cover on the magazine from issue 11 onwards, despite the entire magazine remaining in A5 size, presumably in the hopes of grabbing more attention from children. Unfortunately, the damage from losing the older fans took its toll on the magazine, and it was cancelled in March 2014 with issue 13 being the final issue.

But this isn't the end of Pokémon magazines in the UK. On 29 March 2017, Immediate Media published its own magazine. Known simply as *Pokémon*, the Immediate Media iteration is in many ways similar to Future's magazine with a few differences in how the content is handled, such as including stickers in every issue, or the artwork section featuring children showing their collection as well as their artwork and being limited to a single page. Perhaps due to the boost supplied by *Pokémon Go*, this magazine has proven to be the most successful with over thirty editions in existence.

As a side note, it's always worth taking a gander at the magazines, if not for the content then just for the free item. Sometimes this is more along the lines of a (sample) packet of cards, but at other times, they're more 'exclusive', such as a Squirtle squirter or a set of pin badges. I also recommend you take a peek at the French magazine if you're ever in France, since their magazines often have different freebies and posters to the UK and are mainly exclusive as well.

Known by fans as Retsuden stampers, these blind packaged stamps made by Ensky in Japan feature a wide range of Pokémon. Collectors of individual Pokémon are particularly fond of these, and will go so far as to buy entire lots in a bid to track down their favourites.

Stamp 151, later rebranded as Pocket Monsters Stamp with the arrival of the Johto Pokémon, are non-inked stamps featuring a small Pokémon figure at the top to show who the stamp is at the bottom. Some of these saw multiple releases on different coloured bases.

Known as Character Stamps in Japanese with the English subtitle of Pocket Monsters Stamp Collection, these stamps are similar to Stamp 151 in some ways. The figures are different to those shown on Stamp 151, and they are self-inking. The colour bases are a good indication of what series each one comes from.

Other notable lines from Japan include Battle Museum, Full Color Stadium and Chou Get.

A collection of Retsuden Stampers, including special edition Shaymin. Some special edition releases, such as the glittery Shaymin stamper seen here, will appear from time to time in special sets. These are an ongoing series, with the latest series including Pokémon from Ultra Sun and Ultra Moon.

Selection of Stamp 151s (Pocket Monster Stamps). The Squirtle at the top right who sits upon a silver base is a special edition.

An assortment of character stamps.

Chapter Two
Other Merchandise

In July 1998, All Nippon Airways (ANA) unleashed its very first Pokémon jets. Decked out with Pikachu and some of his friends, the flight included exclusive merchandise onboard, as well as a true Pokémon-themed flying experience. In the years that followed, the jet was repainted several times to include newer Pokémon, and collectibles for these jets were in no short supply. Even if you were unable to fly on one yourself, many airports and even regular stores stocked replica planes and other merchandise.

Catching a flight on one of these jets is a longtime dream for many, but for those who have yet to fly, you may be out of luck for a while. In 2016 ANA painted over its final Pokémon jet, giving the reasonable explanation that the jet used was an older aircraft and no longer truly suitable. But there's a glimmer of hope – ANA has stated that this is not the end for the Pokémon jumbo jets just yet.

A popular collectible in any franchise, Pokémon badges exist in a variety of sizes from plenty of different locations. The most prominent

A collection of ANA collectibles (back to front, left to right: pencil case, moving plane set, postcard, model, foam squeeze, pen).

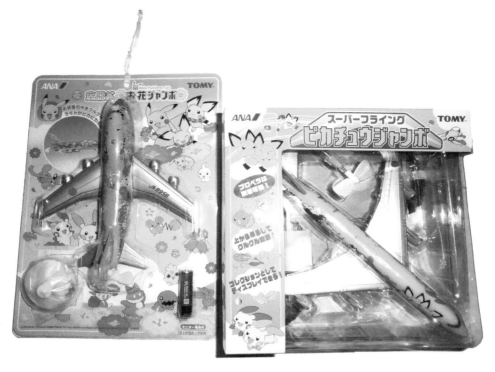

Two larger ANA models.

Can badge selection. The giant can badge here is from a tin, where it doubles as a lid. In the UK, our badges frequently originate from greetings cards (such as the Pikachu on the top right) or from companies that deal with pop culture. The badge featuring Ash and Pikachu came with some early Hasbro figure sets known as Grabber Balls.

can badges are from Japan, where several different series exist. Some contain a randomised can badge in a pack whilst some are available directly from Pokémon Centers.

Like can badges, pin badges are highly collectable, and more have surfaced over the recent years. In the UK, our current most prominent method of obtaining pin badges is through the Trading Card Game, where sets often come with a pin badge included.

As a heads up, the Pokémon Center is the primary source of most pin badges, and holiday releases are always limited to that specific year. It's not uncommon to find pin badges dedicated to the games, either.

Monster Ball Badges are another pin badge you might come across in Japanese auction sites or recycle stores. Created by Media Factory, these pins come in a PokéBall (Monster Ball in Japan) case. This isn't limited to the standard PokéBall, however, and other balls, such as Master Balls, could also be obtained.

Shiny Pokémon. Every fan knows that shiny Pokémon are rare (well, unless you have a cheat device, but that doesn't count here). In terms of collectibles, shiny Pokémon are mostly every bit as elusive as the in-game shinies themselves. However, there has been retail merchandise of shiny Pokémon released in the past, and no doubt

Pin badge selection. The Celebi, Mega Lucario, Froakie and Fennekin pins shown came with the Trading Card Game. The boxed Blastoise and Pidgeotto originate from Korea, but several were released in the UK. The Pokémon Silver and Pokémon Blue pins are from a special gift set in Japan and contained pins of the other games that were available at the time. Pokémon Cooking Club was a Pokémon Center pin from the Johto era, and Ash's Treecko was a retail release in Japan, as is the Pewter City Gym (Nibi City Gym in Japan) set.

Pokémon Center pins. Here we can see a variety of those pin badges, plus a New Year's pin badge featuring the Sinnoh starter Pokémon.

Monster Ball badges. For those wondering, yes, that is indeed Ash's shiny Noctowl.

Shiny Pokémon collectibles (back to front, left to right: Shiny Entei PokéDoll, regular Garchomp Moncolle, shiny Garchomp Moncolle, shiny Latios Kid, shiny Ash's Noctowl pin, shiny Entei, Suicune and Raikou charm set, shiny Entei puzzle). Most of the shiny Pokémon merchandise is, as you may expect, locked behind a lottery of some sort, such as the shiny Entei PokéDoll that can be seen here. It's not always the common Pokémon that have shiny merchandise out there – Garchomp received a shiny Monster Collection figure, seen here with the regular release, as part of a short promotion.

there will be in the future. Whatever the form of obtainment, be it retail or prize, expect to shell out a lot of money for certain items in this category.

One other thing – Pokémon has a wide range of collectibles that aren't what most people would think of when they hear the word. Pokémon toilet paper is definitely one of the more well-known novelty items out there. How about a Lure Keychain featuring Slowpoke and his tail? Remember, it will grow back. Even the UK saw a bit of the randomness – a gumball machine (missing the lid unfortunately) and a camera, which automatically prints out a Pokémon-themed border when the film is printed. It might not seem that impressive now, but back when Photoshop and digital cameras were relatively new, they were a fun novelty.

Also, be on the lookout for some of the items that are inspired by the anime. These can be fun novelties, and a lot of collectors are always on the lookout for them, especially for characters such as the Squirtle Squad. If there's a character with a large enough presence and a significant difference to others of its kind, there's a high chance that at least one collectible will have been made at some point.

Pikachu gumball machine, Slowpoke Lure keychain, Pikachu camera and Pokémon toilet paper. Pokémon bog roll? Yep, that's what's wrapped up here.

Mew with Ancient Mew tablet strap, anime Jigglypuff Kids figure, Squirtle Squad lock, Skitty TV.

Going to the beach? Whilst some of these items are on the rarer side, if you're the type of Pokémaniac who likes to go all out, you might enjoy the selection of items featured in this book.

Need to spruce up your computer? Over the years, Pokémon has amassed a range of items for the tech wizards out there. In the UK, this mostly consists of mouse mats, which were more available during the early days of Kanto and Johto's reign. In Japan, computer mats pop up from time to time, and Buffalo released a Piplup (and Pikachu) mouse and matching mouse mat back during the days of Sinnoh's release.

Pokémon boogie board, inflatable ring, Pikachu beach ball, Ultra Ball beach ball and Diamond/Pearl bucket and spade set. The Pikachu boogie board gives new meaning to Surfing Pikachu and was available in the UK, as was the Ultra Ball inflatable. Other balls are also available and, if you're looking towards Japan, there's a good chance your favourite ball exists in inflatable ball form too. The other items are from Japan, and were available during the Diamond and Pearl era. Yes, you can get a Pokémon paddling pool over there, too.

Pokémon computer mat, mouse mat and Piplup mouse.

Chapter Three
Kanto

The region that started it all. Kanto features a wide variety of popular Pokémon, including fan favourites such as Pikachu, Eevee, Charizard, Bulbasaur, Blastoise, Mew, Snorlax and many, many more. It goes without saying that many of the monsters from this generation have merchandise that far outweighs Pokémon from other regions, even if they were considered unpopular.

One of the things that stands out about this generation is how some of the merchandise was created before the anime series aired. Due to this, some character models are different in comparison to the character models we see today.

Let's take a closer look at a couple of earlier designs. The earliest of Mew merchandise was pure white with only a hint of pink here and there, as opposed to being pure pink as he is today. The plushes featuring white Mew are only present in the earliest of Pokémon

Pokédex and Bulbasaur, Charmander and Squirtle money banks. Here, we can see the starters using their original appearance. Most noticeably, Charmander has a spike on his back, a trait seen exclusively in early products. Squirtle's shell is also closer to that of his shiny appearance, and Bulbasaur's colouration is somewhat different to most of his later merchandise.

Mew and 1998 Mew UFO Catcher plush toys. By the way, the small plush on the right (aside from being not to scale, approx. 3 in.) is a Suzunari 'bell' plush, a line of tiny plushes with velvet material and little bells on them. Cute, right? You probably won't say that when you learn that most of these plushies are very sought-after and can reach $100 just for one.

collectibles, including the Monster Collection 'Tomy' Mew figure that was released in the UK.

Pikachu's difference, whilst not as drastic, is one that still divides some fans today – he was much more rotund, and this chubby appearance is preferred by some collectors. Extremely early merchandise also sees Pikachu with a white stomach, something which returned in the *Detective Pikachu* movie.

On the subject of Pikachu, let's address the elephant (or mouse) in the room.

Pikachu. Whether you love or hate him, there's no denying that collectibles featuring Pikachu are everywhere. Originally, the spot for

2017 Pikachu TY Beanie vs original 1998 Pikachu UFO Catcher and reversible plush.

mascot was to be awarded to Clefairy, though Pikachu won out in the end and thus, if you're looking to start a collection of Pikachu, I have fantastic news for you – it's easy to amass a large collection of Pikachu items. I'm not even trying, and I still seem to find the electric mouse zapping his way into my house. That's not to say that Pikachu collectibles are worthless or anything like that. Sometimes, it's quite the contrary. A lot of earlier Pikachu merchandise was mass-produced and this has affected resale value for many items both in the UK and in Japan, where you can easily pick up a lot of earlier Pikachu items for a very modest price.

Still, there are fans out there who believe that it's time for Pikachu to be given a rest, which is understandable given that Pikachu rarely wins top place in popularity contests run by fans or even official companies. Pokémon #25 is certainly a polarising character when it comes to collectibles, and sometimes even the games.

A collection of Pikachu plush toys.

But perhaps something is changing, even if just a little bit. With the release of *Pokémon Let's Go! Pikachu* and *Let's Go! Eevee*, a new secondary mascot seems to be coming.

Eevee, the evolution Pokémon, has been a fan favourite since the very beginning. With the ability to evolve into a number of different Pokémon, Eevee has been a prominent face on merchandise since the earliest Kanto days. Collectibles featuring Eevee and its evolutions are prone to fetching high prices and starting fierce bidding wars, and it seems like this little bundle of fluff's rising popularity is challenging Pikachu's top spot now more than ever.

Locating Eevee merchandise shouldn't be too much of a problem for anyone, there being a huge selection of Eevee collectibles in existence. In Japan, Eevee has become the star of several limited promotions for Pokémon Centers, often being accompanied by Jolteon, Flareon, Vaporeon, Espeon, Umbreon, Leafeon, Glaceon and Sylveon. Here in the UK, Eevee is becoming more prominent with collectibles, often appearing alongside Pikachu in various box sets and individual series.

Although it's highly unlikely that Eevee will ever become the new face of Pokémon after over twenty years of the mascot being cemented as Pikachu, it's nice knowing that even Pikachu has a rival out there.

When Pokémon first hit our shores, you couldn't walk into a shop without being confronted by a wall of Pokémon goods. Some of the most prominent items during their original release included the Tomy Battle Figures we mentioned earlier (Monster Collection), Basic Plushes (Jigglypuff, Psyduck and Gengar) and Beanies (Eevee and Meowth).

A collection of Eevee items – A 30 cm LED Lamp, Tomy plush, PokéDoll plush, early Tomy plush, keychain plush, clear Kids figure, First Edition Trading Figure, Slider, 'Grabber' figure.

These plastered the walls of every store, and sold like hot cakes during the Pokémon craze. Items that rolled out a bit later include jumbo plush (Pikachu, and a Meowth was also available), Candy Keepers plush (Charizard), Decorative Ornaments (Eevee and Charmander), Applause Battle plush (Vulpix) and a selection of children's watches. Looking for adult watches? Head on over to Japan – they've got you covered. Not pictured but worth mentioning are Hasbro talking figures with some, such as Meowth, being sold with Japanese and English voices in the UK and without a discernible way to tell them apart aside from letting them speak, and Play-by-Play plushes, a line that was mostly known for appearing in amusement arcades and for some being hilariously off-model.

Pokémon marbles were intended to be the next big collectible, and they were a hit. All 151 Pokémon were given a marble in this series, maximising the collecting potential. A large PokéBall case, PokéBall shooters with a Charizard or Blastoise motif, collector pouches and hard cases were released, featuring a variety of different Pokémon. Collector pouches of Raichu, Arcanine and Beedrill were also planned and prototypes were seen in advertisements, but they were ultimately transformed into the plastic marble cases instead.

A selection of early Pokémon merchandise.

Above left: Large PokéBall marble container and marble launcher plus Hitmonchan, Cubone, Raichu and Zapdos marble cases.

Above right: A selection of marble pouches.

The pouches were intended to be the main selling point for the marbles, and each included two power marbles (metallic) and eight crystal marbles (see-through). A special edition Mew marble was distributed via Toys R Us stores on a cardboard backing, and a small selection of blind packs were available for a limited time. There were three series of marble pouches available, and each character could be obtained in every colour shown here.

Tiger was the main handler of electronics in the UK, and from the company came many different games and gadgets. Shown here are a few games by Tiger Electronics: the *PokéBall* LCD game, *Thundershock Challenge* pinball game and the lesser known *I Choose You!* game. Many of Tiger's products were widely available during the days of Kanto, and are some of the most recognisable toys from that era.

Here we can see another set of Tiger toys that were available during the initial UK release. These yo-yos light up and play a tune as they are being used, featuring semi-3D portraits of several Pokémon. Some of these yo-yos are relatively simple to track down, whilst others, such as Marowak, are more elusive.

These light-up keychains sadly have non-replaceable batteries, but you can get a pretty good amount of flashes out of them before they retire. These little figures were once abundant on shelves everywhere, taking entire rows all for themselves. As with a lot of Pokémon merchandise, you can still find them occasionally in

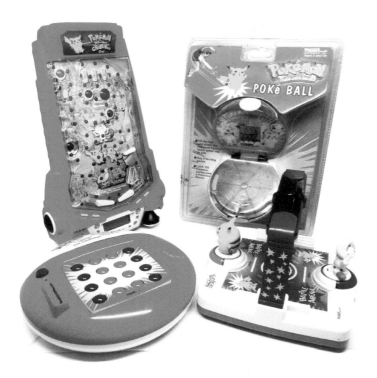

Tiger Pokémon games.

Electronic Yo-Yos. Not shown are Pikachu, Meowth and Jigglypuff.

Light-up keychains.

their original packaging, but finding them out of their packets is much easier. As a side note, some were released in Japan, with a very slight change to their bottom switch. I know that Wobbuffet and Togepi are from Johto and technically shouldn't be in a Kanto photograph – but this is also a good way of showing you some of the Japan releases, including the former, which was never found over here.

Hasbro took advantage of Pokémon's popularity by teaming up with other companies to produce Pokémon-themed versions of equally popular family games, such as *Monopoly*, *Yahtzee Jr* and (obliterator of friendships) *Sorry!*. *Monopoly* would later see another Kanto release in 2014 where, instead of buying locations, you buy Pokémon. Both versions of *Monopoly* include an alternate release. In the US, the re-release *Monopoly* included additional tokens for Cubone, Magikarp, Psyduck and Meowth.

The *Master Trainer* game was also released in Japan, and the games feature tokens of all 151 Pokémon. *Power Pairs* is exactly what you expect it to be, only the counters are in the shape of PokéBalls. The *Pokémon Adventure Jr* game was created by Wizards, the then-holders of the Pokémon Trading Card Game. As the name would suggest, it is geared towards younger players.

Another popular item from the early days are Power Bouncers, known in Japan as Super Balls. What's interesting about the figures contained within these bouncy balls is that in Japan some of them could also be found outside the balls as parts of other series. Once again, Togepi is here since you could buy Togepi much earlier than you could other Johto Pokémon, with Togepi being the first Johto Pokémon to ever hit our shores.

Hasbro board games. The original *Monopoly* could feature regular pewter playing pieces, with the latter edition being shown here.

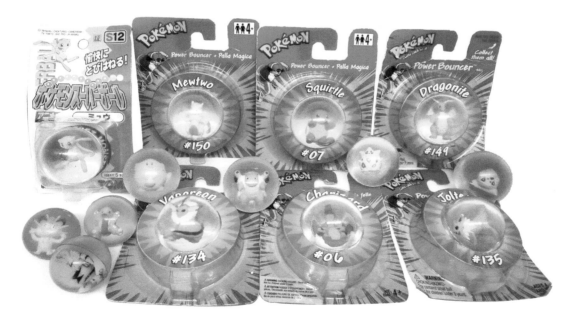

Pokémon Power Bouncers (and others). You might notice three other oddly coloured bouncy balls. These aren't part of this set, but it's worth knowing that Japan had other series' as well, which featured Pokémon that never received their own Power Bouncer. These were usually Pokémon that were not considered 'popular' overseas.

Another of Hasbro's offerings, the Pokémon Playsets are frequently compared to Polly Pocket, and even listed as such. Although they share no affiliation with the brand, these playsets are still considered popular enough that the search phrase 'Pokémon Polly Pocket' is used more often than the title of each set. These were also released in Japan, and both countries saw more sets released down the line.

One figure in particular that collectors consider desirable is the pink Rhyhorn, a reference to the anime episode 'In the Pink' ('The Island of Pink Pokémon' in Japan).

Popular stationery company RoseArt was also in on the Pokémon 'fad' of the 1990s and produced a variety of stationery kits. Some of these items crossed over into other sets (the sticker album comes to mind), but many of the colouring sheets and accessories are, for the most part, only available in one set. Since colouring sheets are typically used immediately, finding a kit or box complete is more of a challenge than locating, say, the Battle Pack figures still in their box. Other companies also challenged RoseArt's products, such as Toy Island.

Arena Adventure and Park Adventure sets.

Assorted RoseArt sets, crayons and felt tips.

Toy Island Gel Pens. Toy Island produced several different lines of Pokémon stationery goods, but shied away from colouring pages and sticker sheets and opted instead for more practical products such as these gel pens.

Bathroom equipment was abundant back in the days of Red and Blue. The Gameboy bubble bath holder tends to bring memories flooding back to those around for this era, particularly as preceding editions in this format also include other Nintendo hits such as Donkey Kong Country. Whilst it can't be seen from this angle, Meowth comes with a suction cup attached to the back, though the heaviness of the model sometimes causes it to fall off regardless. The Pikachu toothbrush holder and toothbrush combo is a staple of bathroom items, as is the Pikachu bubble bath container. Finally, Pokémon toothbrushes featuring several of the more popular characters were released, and were one of the few lines to continue into the Johto era.

Pokémon Pikachu, or as it's known in Japan, *Pocket Pikachu*, was a pedometer and game featuring the popular electric mouse. To put it simply, the more you walked, the more Watts you could gain, and the

Assorted Pokémon items for the bathroom.

Pokémon Pikachu, Pocket Pikachu Color and Pokémon Pikachu Color.

happier Pikachu would be because you can exchange these Watts to play games. Ignore Pikachu for too long, and he'll walk out on you. You monster.

Although technically part of the Johto Region's releases, *Pokémon Pikachu 2* was upgraded to a full colour game and compatibility with *Pokémon Gold/Silver*'s Daily Gift mechanic.

Although these pins aren't too difficult to track down, finding a specific pin is an entirely different matter. These pin badges are packed five to a set, but there's also a little catch – Pikachu is in every set. Factory boxes of these pins also do not seem to be randomised too well, so a factory case may end up containing mostly the same assortment of twenty-five or so characters. Thankfully, with pin trading on the rise, there's a good chance you'll find other collectors willing to trade theirs for others in the set.

Of course, some series see a release so limited that many people aren't even aware of their existence. Such is the case with Pokémon Micro Machines. These mini playsets came with three small Pokémon figures, a small play area and a PokéBall containing another mystery Pokémon figure inside.

Only two sets have been found: Celadon City (mystery Pokémon is Psyduck) and Cinnabar Island (mystery Pokémon is still unknown). The full series would have included a total of eight sets which include Cerulean City, Route 3, Viridian Forest, Viridian City, Route 2 and Fuschia City (misspelt as 'Fushia City'), in addition to the Pokémon Island Battle Arena Playset.

A selection of 2000 Collector Pins. Here we can see another series which included all of the Kanto Region Pokémon. This set of pin badges was released in Sydney in 2000. Despite this, select badges were given away free with at least one magazine in the UK. Years later, overstock saw them making their way over to resellers in the UK.

Micro Machines Celadon City set.

Pokémon Micro Machines backing.

Unfortunately, little else is known about this set, or even what the other mystery Pokémon were to be. Even if you do locate one of the figures, you might not actually have a piece from the Micro Machines sets. Instead, you may have just located one of Hasbro's Mystery Figures.

These small figures were released in a small bag featuring Hasbro's signature red packaging and usually contained two figures inside a clear packet at random. The packet also wrote the individual number of the Pokémon as stated by the Pokédex, and all 151 Pokémon were up for grabs. These figures use the same mould as some that are found in Japan, but the figure quality is somewhat different.

Meanwhile in Japan, an even bigger assortment of collectibles were being produced (as is to be expected, really). Some of these collectibles are almost identical to the ones produced overseas, such as the Moncolle figures mentioned earlier. Some deviated a little from the original Japanese product, while others were completely unique to the country.

Rare flocked versions of some characters exist, but these remove the money slot. Other limited variants include glow in the dark and glow in the dark stamper sets.

Hasbro Mystery Figures.

56

A selection of Japanese Pokémon boxes. Seen here are a few of the Kanto sets that could be found in the country.

Japanese Pokémon items. First off, we have a PokéBall dispenser for a decorative Pokémon sticker tape. Next is a Blastoise v. Dragonite diorama model. Then we have a projector, not unlike those which you see in the UK. Finally, we have one of the earliest figure boxes, Pokémon Field, which features connecting parts to put together a whole set of minigames once completed. A few more items that could be found during the earlier days include this set of cards and two game books. The top comes with a talking Pikachu (and some nice illustrations of Eevee and Vaporeon, telling a tale certainly never seen in the anime), and the second contains figures of Pikachu, Bulbasaur, Charmander, Squirtle, Pidgeotto and Butterfree (Ash's Pokémon in the anime at that point in time).

Kanto Money Banks (back to front, left to right: Raichu, Articuno, Zapdos, Moltres, Mewtwo, Venusaur, Vulpix, Eevee, Cubone). These small plastic money banks made by Banpresto feature a good selection of Pokémon, though they are once again exclusive to Japan. They aren't too rare, but more popular characters such as Vulpix or the legendary birds might mean you'll have to fork over a bit more cash to add them to your collection.

Mew Money Bank variants.

These small can badges were available in Pokémon Centers back in 2001. They feature artwork created by trading card game artists and, as their name suggests, all 151 Pokémon are part of this set. The badge illustrations are not really found in other products, making them highly collectible. If you're aiming for the full set, you might want to look into purchasing the special hanger that was also created to display the set.

Speaking of badges, for the third anniversary, this set of pin badges was available. Limited to 4,000 pieces and presented in a clear plastic case, these individually numbered sets make a wonderful focal point for the dedicated pin collector, providing fans with three different milestones that Pokémon had achieved at that point in time.

A series that's relatively unheard of, Pracoro is a dice game that appeared in Japan, but only for Kanto Pokémon. What makes Pracoro so collectible has to be the dice themselves, which are modelled after certain Pokémon.

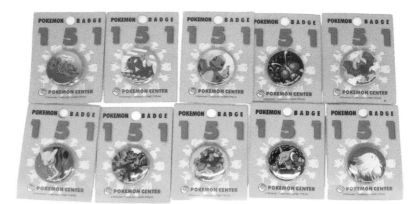

Selection of
Pokémon
151 badges.

Pocket Monsters
third anniversary
Memorial Pin
set, featuring
Pikachu, Venusaur,
Charizard and
Blastoise.

Squirtle Pracoro box, plus assorted Pracoro dice. The dice at the back are around 1 in., but the
dice in front are a tiny 0.5 cm. It's hard to see the ones at the front, which are Zapdos, Squirtle,
Poliwhirl, Machop, Scyther, Electabuzz, Scyther (alternate), Wigglytuff, Meowth, Gyrados and
Abra, whilst at the back we have Charmeleon, Ivysaur, Wartortle, Electabuzz, Lickitung, Abra,
Kadabra and Alakazam.

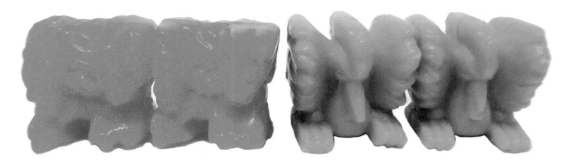

A close-up of the tiny Ponyta and Moltres Pracoro dice. What should be noted is that the tiny dice come in multiple poses, which can be difficult to spot from a distance. Notice how one Ponyta has an open mouth and how one Moltres has an open mouth and one slightly raised claw? These tiny differences can only be seen up close most of the time, making it somewhat difficult to discern which version (or indeed, which Pokémon) are included in certain lots.

Slowbro Christmas tree tail decoration. In Japan, even Slowbro dresses up for Christmas. This approximately 6-inch-tall figure is sure to get a laugh out of the people who see it. Even those not interested in collecting Slowbro tend to include this on their wishlist!

Chapter Four
Johto

It was around the time of Johto's arrival that the initial Pokémon 'fad' had wound down. Many people were selling off their trading cards and toys, leaving only the most loyal of fans to hold a collection. New merchandise had slowed to a crawl and companies were offering heavy discounts on their Pokémon collectibles and trading cards, assuming that the franchise would soon disappear into obscurity, like many crazes. But this was just the UK – in Japan, Pokémon still boasted a tremendous amount of merchandise. Perhaps it's no wonder that certain Johto collectibles can be very difficult to track down, with many people choosing to find new brands to focus on around this time.

Johto saw only a limited release on long-time popular items such as plush toys, where only the stars of *Pikachu's Rescue Adventure* saw the light of day in the UK. The usual obligatory items such as books and puzzles were about, as were some more unusual items such as toothbrushes and cake frill. Hasbro released the giant electronic Lugia figure to coincide with *Pokémon the Movie 2000*, and a very limited amount of Power Bouncers with Johto Pokémon were floating around

Deluxe PokéDex and life-size Chikorita, Cyndaquil and Totodile plush.

Assorted Johto collectibles.

the UK. Later, the UK also received the overstock from the US, and a small amount of figures from Hasbro's combat range were available in stores for a limited time. Mostly, Pokémon collectibles had dwindled down dramatically.

Locating Johto collectibles in the UK is arguably one of the trickiest of endeavours. As mentioned before, the craze was winding down, and stores were more interested in discounting their Pokémon goods as opposed to risking new items. With this in mind, the Johto editions of *Monopoly*, *Master Trainer* and *Sorry!* took a hit with this, with very few stores choosing to stock them. The original Johto *Monopoly* is the rarest of the four Pokémon *Monopoly* games.

But it wasn't all doom and gloom. For the fans that preferred the more obscure collectibles, Calypso cartons were available, as was the ever-popular Heinz pasta in tomato sauce. In fact, they came in two different tin variations: a shiny label, which was the original release, and a regular label. You could also purchase Mini Lunch Boxes with 'Pokémon' bubblegum (although mine just featured regular bubblegum with no patterns or distinguishing marks whatsoever). Tracking some of these items down isn't the easiest task, particularly as they appeared during a time when Pokémon was no longer considered popular or collectible.

The marbles continued into the Johto Region, but they are significantly rarer. These pouches were available in Gold and Silver

Pokémon *Sorry!* Johto edition.

Mini Lunch Box featuring Ash, Pikachu and Chikorita, Calypso Berry Blast drink cartons featuring Togepi and Granbull and Heinz Pokémon pasta shapes in tomato sauce featuring Lugia and others.

Johto marble pouches and marbles.

colours only, and lasted only one series before retiring, taking the main marble line with it. Locating the Johto marbles is very difficult, and they can reach high prices when on auction. Unlike the Kanto marbles series, only the pouches were ever released.

An attempt to start off a new craze, Pokémon Staks magnets saw a much better release after being sold near their trading card cousins. With 250 Pokémon to collect plus some additional holo Staks featuring the human cast of the show (and of course, Pikachu), trading Staks was almost inevitable in order to complete one's collection. The series made a brief return in the Hoenn Region, but like many Pokémon collectibles, they were not widely sold in the UK and are considered much rarer than the Johto release.

A new addition to the games that this region introduced for the first time were shiny Pokémon, as we covered a bit earlier. These Pokémon had an incredibly low chance of appearing as a wild Pokémon in the games, save for a shiny Gyarados that could be found at the Lake of Rage. As far as merchandising goes, as also mentioned earlier, shiny Pokémon began as a rarity, with most companies preferring to take the safe option of a regularly coloured Charizard. Yet Hasbro took the plunge and released a series of Shining Pokémon figures. Spinarak, Scyther, Cyndaquil, Zapdos, Pikachu and Heracross were also part of this set.

For the release of *Heart Gold* and *Soul Silver*, additional Johto merchandise was produced. The most prominent were the PokéBall Twister figures, featuring the legendary beast trio and final starter evolutions (among others), and a new selection of Kids figures (known here as Soft Figures). Some of these sets lasted for only a short while before they were replaced with other products.

Pokémon Staks.

Hasbro Shiny Pokémon Combat Battle Figures.

In Japan, things were still going well for our Pocket Monster friends as well. The Pokémon Center store made the leap to online shopping, with items available exclusively through them. In stores and arcades, Pokémon were still making their presence known with a wide variety of toys and collectibles sprawling on shelves. Even today, however, many Johto collectibles are considered rarer than the other generations.

Meganium and Raikou PokéBall Twister Figures and Soft Figures (Pokémon Kids) set.

A selection of Japanese items from the Johto era.

The money banks returned for the Johto Region, but they have always been much more difficult to track down in contrast to the Kanto release, which are relatively available. The final starters are very sought after by collectors, regardless of their flocked or regular release.

It should be noted that some Pokémon deviate a little from the normal design, and one Johto Pokémon is the perfect example of this.

Pichu has two well-known different character appearances: Spiky-Ear Pichu (also known as Gizamimi or Notch Ear Pichu) and Tufty Pichu (a fan name given to the Pichu brother with a tuft of fur atop his head). These two variations received a small amount of collectibles after their individual releases, and Tufty Pichu in

Johto Money Banks (left to right: Chikorita, Feraligatr, Cyndaquil, Totodile, Meganium, Bellossom and Blissey).

Spiky-Eared Pichu PokéDoll and Tufty Pichu PokéDoll.

particular is very desirable, with his PokéDoll often fetching very high prices on auction. Other items featuring Tufty also do well on the market.

Another item that you may encounter on Japanese auction sites are these figural keychains. Not only are they fantastic quality, but they include some poses not seen all that often (such as Larvitar, Umbreon and Snubbull).

Johto keychain assortment.

Chapter Five
Hoenn

In the UK, *Pokémon Ruby* and *Sapphire* (known by many as the advanced generation) saw an attempt to bring back the Pokémon craze by flooding stores with new merchandise. Whilst it was never able to reach the popularity of previous games, it did bring with it a host of new collectables for fans, ranging from the usual plush and figure sets to the not-so-usual Metal Tags and Chipz series.

The advanced generation is notably the first time that people in the UK have been able to buy PokéDolls in the UK, even if they weren't labelled as such. Bandai distributed the most merchandise (in terms of most widely available at least), including the import of certain large Tomy figures such as the Absol seen here. Jakks Pacific also joined in later on, including its own ranges of figures, both electronic and regular. As mentioned earlier, this generation also saw a very brief return of the

Hoenn PokéDex, Treecko, Torchic and Mudkip trading figures.

Sliders series, though the only new moulds were that of Treecko, Torchic and Mudkip. For the picky collectors, Treecko has no colouring under his chin and, as you can see in the picture, the gills on Mudkip were not painted on the actual cheek.

One interesting feature of some of the main Bandai toys was their interlocking capability. Other electronic figures include Deoxys and Rayquaza, whilst another line of figures included Aggron and Grovyle. Due to a shorter production, Salamence and Rayquaza are significantly rarer than the other figures in this set.

A selection of Hoenn merchandise.

Charizard and Salamence talking figures. A rather large playset that came packaged with an exclusive Groudon figure could be combined with other figures, such as the Charizard and Salamence seen here.

As with several other series, Europe saw the release of some figures which those of us in the UK never saw. One of these lines is the 'Data Card' line by Bandai. Absol, Kyogre and Groudon were all available in this set, although Absol is by far the most in-demand, and for some collectors, enters Grail-level territory due to how few stores actually sold the item, even in Europe.

Metal Tags and Chipz were one of the new 'Gotta catch 'em all' sets for the third generation. Metal Tags came with the hefty goal of collecting all Pokémon in the National Dex at the time, with packets retailing for £2.99 and containing two random tags and a ball chain, which could either be short or long. Chipz, on the other hand, weren't quite so ambitious. At seventy Chipz, these poker chips had a smaller set list than Metal Tags, but instead relied on rare chase inserts. The rarest of these is a gold Jirachi coin, which was roughly one per factory box (twenty-four packets). Silver chase Chipz could also be pulled, but these were roughly two to three per factory box.

Absol Data Card figure.

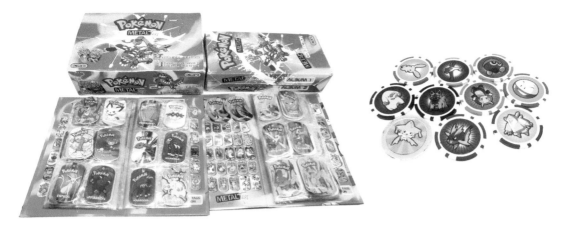

Metal Tags (left) and Chipz (right).

Meanwhile, in playgrounds across the UK, a new Pokémon craze was starting: Pokémon Waps. These small plastic disc-like toys were all the rage once upon a time, fetching high prices online as fans desperately tried to complete their sets, and other fans clambered to get their favourite Pokémon in as many different colours as possible. In other European countries, a similar item known as Kraks was released. One major difference between the two is that Kraks do not have holos.

V-Trainers were originally released for the Johto era, but also saw new releases in Hoenn. These figures could interact with a larger device, though most collectors prefer the smaller packs with more figure variety. Perhaps in the same way that most Hoenn Sliders were re-releases, V-Trainers were given the same treatment, but with updated characters, such as Team Magma.

As is the case with any series, some V-Trainer figures were never produced, though prototypes were made.

Assorted Kraks and Waps.

Pokémon V-Trainer Team Magma set with Suicune and Raichu (other figures left to right: Alakazam, Feraligatr, Raikou and Sentret).

Prototype V-Trainer figures Blastoise and Umbreon. Being one of the most popular Pokémon, the latter is widely sought after, since only a few prototypes exist. The Blastoise has an incorrectly coloured chin.

Data Carrier Pokémon figures are one of the many figure sets released in Japan during this time. They are notable for being slightly larger than usual figures, standing at approximately 2.5 in. The figures are compatible with the titular Data Carrier module that can be seen here, though most collectors prefer to stick with their favourite Pokémon figures (at least in the UK). Since the series includes some more popular characters, such as Manectric, Absol and Salamance, these figures are often desirable.

Also released during this generation was the PokéPark! No, not the Wii game. The PokéPark was a fully fledged Pokémon theme park in Japan (and later in Taiwan), and the first theme park in the world purely dedicated to a videogame. Featuring a Rayquaza coaster, Latios and Latias pirate ship and an Entei, Suicune and Raikou carousel amongst other Pokémon-themed rides, PokéPark was Pokémon's answer to Disneyland. The park moved to Taiwan in June 2005 before closing in September 2006.

Pokémon's tenth anniversary took place in 2006, though it went largely unnoticed overall in the UK. The vast majority of merchandise produced in English for the celebration was available in the US in Target stores (such as this Lugia figure) and via their Pokémon Center. The UK did receive a small event although, cards excluded, the only piece of merchandise you could really take away from it was a colouring sheet for a contest that was held. Since these are mostly throwaway items, they're difficult to track down these days.

Data Carrier including Groudon and Manectric figures (other figures left to right: Absol, Mudkip, Salamence, Blastoise and Rayquaza).

PokéPark Nintendo DS, strap and keychain. At one stage, the PokéPark DS console shown here was offered to other companies for resale after the park closed down, but it wasn't long before they sold out. The strap shown attached to the DS in this photograph did not come with the DS, and was available separately. These days, PokéPark merchandise doesn't pop up all that frequently, and competition for certain items can be fierce.

Tenth anniversary Lugia figure.

Chapter Six
Sinnoh

Diamond and *Pearl* always hold fond memories for me, in part due to it being the game of the moment when I first visited Japan after years of yearning to travel there. It was also around this time that Pokémon received a surge of new and returning collectors, and thus has arguably the most amount of documented merchandise. Collectibles from this era vary drastically in worth, and some tend to be easier to locate than, say, Hoenn or Johto items.

Merchandise in the UK soared once again during the Sinnoh era, with a large range of new collectibles hitting the market. Jakks Pacific unleashed more figures that were more readily available than before, and added some electronic talking plushes to the mix, although as with many series, the UK skipped several waves of the plush, and often sold off the excess stock from the US. Among other items, Bandai continued its line of PokéBall and spinning figures and introduced the Ultimate Battle Thinkchip device, as well as some other lines with a focus on marbles.

Sinnoh PokéDex with Turtwig, Chimchar and Piplup PokéDolls.

An assortment of *Diamond* and *Pearl* merchandise.

Unlike most previous generations, the Sinnoh generation produced some more crafty kits, such as door hangers and window stickers that were released by Totum. A wall hook by Decofun also saw a release here in the UK, featuring Dialga and Palkia. On that note, this generation saw the return of the large sticker boxes and sticker packs, which were more difficult to find in the Johto and Hoenn generations.

A particular favourite among fans, the vehicles seen by Team Rocket in the anime saw a rather brief release in model form. Released by Jakks Pacific, the Meowth Balloon and Magicarp (curiously given the wrong name and not including the full title on the box: Magikarp Submarine) models stand around 8.5 in. and 6.5 in. respectively. Both include an attack mode and storage space.

This generation also marks the end of an era, with the final series of Pokémon Friends being released. These 3–4 in. plushes came packaged with a piece of ramune candy, and had been a staple of Pokémon collecting since 1997 when the first series came out. The final series included characters from the most recent movie at the time, *Pokémon: Giratina and the Sky Warrior*.

Also around this time was the tenth anniversary for the movies. This went largely unnoticed in the UK, but in Japan, it was celebrated

Pokémon sticker box, wall hook, door hanger kit and window stickers kit.

Pokémon Vehicles.

with the release of some very limited collectibles. These special box sets included many main characters from all of the movies that were available at the time (up until Darkrai), and were not available to buy separately. These included a set of pearl finish Moncolle figures featuring Mewtwo, Lugia, Entei, Celebi, Latios, Latias, Absol, Jirachi, Pikachu, Deoxys, Rayquaza, Mew, Lucario, Dialga, Darkrai, Palkia and Manaphy, a finger puppet set that included Mewtwo, Lugia, Entei,

Shaymin Pokémon Friends box and Buneary Friends plush.

Pokémon Movie tenth anniversary Monster Collection figure set.

Celebi, Latios with Latias, Darkrai, Manaphy, Lucario, Deoyxs and Jirachi, a trading card set and a double-sided board game.

This board game included cards of nearly every Pokémon that had appeared in a movie until that point. The other side features a game based on *Pokémon: The Rise of Darkrai*, the latest movie that was released at the time.

Pokémon Movie tenth anniversary Double Board Game.

Figures from around this era were once bountiful, much more so than other generations. These days, tracking down random sets such as Pokémon Joint Palace might take you some time. But it's admittedly still easier than tracking down most other generations.

Koinobori (carp streamers) are a common sight in Japan, used to celebrate Children's Day. Since their name says it all, it makes sense for there to be a Magikarp (known in Japan as Koiking) one out there, right? This is definitely one of the more unique items to find for your collection, although there are other Pokémon Koinobori out there too.

Hey, it wasn't just Pikachu who received his own tamagotchi-styled collectible. In Japan, Manaphy no Tamago (Manaphy's Egg) was also available.

There were some other fun items released in Japan, too. Pokémon Gumi Factory (the end product tastes delicious by the way), kitchen foil and sandwich bags were just some of the items available at the time. The kitchen foil was exclusive to Pokémon Centers, but the gummy maker and sandwich bags by Takara Tomy could be found in multiple locations across Japan.

Finally, Pokémon Centers around Japan celebrated their tenth anniversary during this generation. To celebrate the occasion, all of the starter Pokémon PokéDolls were re-released in a new minky fabric, with Pikachu's featuring a cute little bowtie. A larger plush of Pikachu wearing a party hat also carried along with him a mini tenth anniversary Pikachu PokéDoll.

Pokémon Joint
Palace set.

Koinobori and Manaphy no Tamago (not to scale).

Pokémon sandwich bags, tin foil and Pokémon Gumi Factory.

Tenth anniversary Pokémon Center collectibles. The large PokéDoll tin seen here came packaged with a PokéDoll bouncy ball. Pikachu, Piplup, Turtwig and Chimchar were available, but only one was supplied in each tin randomly. Other items featuring the tin's design, such as notepads and sticker sheets could also be bought.

Chapter Seven
Unova

Unova features the first games in the series to have two sequels: *Pokémon White 2* and *Pokémon Black 2*, instead of what people assumed would be *Pokémon Gray*. In the UK, Nintendo attempted to market the game by recruiting popular boy band One Direction, although the only collectibles affected by this partnership were a handful of promotional stands and leaflets. Much of the merchandise released during this era was the same as what was released for the Sinnoh Region.

Jakks Pacific was the main retailer of plush toys for this generation. Both Jakks and Bandai released the bulk of merchandise found in the UK overall, with Bandai returning with its spinning PokéBall toys and Jakks bringing back the Throw PokéBalls. As stated earlier in this book, this was also the last region to feature Kids figures in the UK, at least for now.

Unova also featured the (currently) final set of the long-running PokéBall keychain sets. The final series included Scraggy and the middle-starters of the Unova land, bringing an end to this series at a respectable twenty-five sets in total.

Something different that this generation tried out was a larger selection of tiny figures. Whilst it was still possible to purchase larger figures such

Unova PokéDex plus Snivy, Tepig and Oshwawott large Tomy plush.

An assortment of
Black and *White*
collectibles.

Pokémon
keychains,
Wave 25.

as Monster Collection or Kids, Bandai and Jakks Pacific released a set of much smaller figures. The figures came packaged in large boxes and contained a PokéBall, and some also added a box which would snap shut upon the Pokémon's arrival. As with all tiny figures such as these, locating them can be tricky, unless you find one still in the box.

Large figures of Reshiram and Zekrom by Jakks Pacific were released in big window box packaging. The trend of large legendary figures such as these would continue, but the window box packaging would not.

Jakks Pacific smaller figures.

Large Reshiram and Zekrom figures.

From Jakks and CDI, Ash's Travel Pack includes a few items intended for roleplay purposes. Ash's backpack, his gloves, a foam PokéBall and a standard Jakks Pacific Pikachu figure are also perfect for anyone who ran out of time with their Ash Ketchum cosplay.

In the UK, we only saw the release of the Jakks plush toys. As always, Japan featured a much broader selection. In particular, Japan manufactured plush toys of the middle and final evolutions of the starter Pokémon of Oshawott, Tepig and Snivy. Sadly, like with most generations, these never saw their way to UK shelves due to the lack of Pokémon Centers. Some, however, made their way to the US, making them somewhat less rare than others.

Ash's Travel Pack.

Japanese Pokémon Center plush (front to back, left to right: Samurott, Pignite, Dewott, Servine).

Chapter Eight
Kalos

Pokémon X/Y yields the lowest sales for a main Pokémon game thus far, but this does not change the incredible amount of collectibles that were released for the Pokémon featured. This generation also introduced us to Mega Pokémon, many of which were upgraded versions of fan favourites from previous generations. Inspired by the culture of the French, the Kalos Region also marks history for European Pokémon fans. For the first time ever, Europe even had its very own Pokémon Center – Pokémon Center Paris.

Pokémon Center Paris was a pop-up shop that lasted from 4–21 June 2014. The shop sold many of the plushes found on the US branch, complete with updated hang tags with the French names and a CE mark, which had always been the reason given by Pokémon Company International for not shipping outside America. It also sold t-shirts, mugs and trading cards, and offered an insightful view of the game's development process, with original artwork displayed downstairs. For anyone standing outside, a Vivillon with a special PokéBall pattern was able to be downloaded to *Pokémon X* and *Y* games for the first time ever.

The pop-up, however, didn't go quite as planned. The Pokémon Company greatly underestimated the European fans and their inherently deep pockets, as well as how starved they had been for top quality collectibles. Some items, such as the life-size Fennekin plush

Kalos Region PokéDex and Fennekin, Chespin and Froakie Tomy plush.

and Charizard mugs, sold out on the opening day. After less than twenty-four hours of being open, the store had to limit the amount of plush purchases to one per person. The same later happened with the t-shirts, with only kids' sizes being available after forty-eight hours. Despite putting these limits in place, the store's entire stock was depleted after only a week, and only the art gallery remained open.

Nevertheless, it was certainly a sight that European fans wouldn't want to have missed. There's still no word on it returning, unfortunately, though most fans remain optimistic.

Pokémon Center Paris entrance.

Braixen, Quilladin and Frogadier Pokémon Center Paris plush.

Back in the UK, Pokémon merchandise was primarily handled by Tomy, who released large figures of the two main legendaries, Yveltal and Xernas, large plushes of the starters, medium plushes of various other Pokémon such as Litleo and Pumpkaboo, a selection of Moncolle figures with and without additional PokéBalls, and even a Hedbanz board game.

With the introduction of Mega Pokémon, it didn't take too long for the original starters to overshadow the new Pokémon with their new forms. Tomy introduced a line of larger, high quality Battle Attack figures which included Mega Venusaur, Mega Blastoise and Mega Charizard Y. Later, Mega Charizard X would also join this line. These figures weren't on sale for a long period of time, and sold out fairly quickly in comparison to other products on offer.

Later into Kalos's lifeline, a set of Mega Pokémon Danglers saw a release in discount stores. These included both Mega Mewtwo, both Mega Charizard, Mega Garchomp, Mega Absol, Mega Ampharos, Mega Gardevoir, Mega Blaziken and Mega Lucario, and sold for £2.99 a pack. It probably goes without saying that with that kind of price today, they were instant hits and sold out very quickly.

This region also takes place during the twentieth anniversary of Pokémon. The most well-known form of collectibles released was a series that would see a new legendary Pokémon released every month.

An assortment of X and Y merchandise.

Tomy Battle Attack Mega Venusaur, Mega Charizard Y and Mega Blastoise figures.

Tomy Mega Pokémon Danglers.

Keldeo twentieth anniversary set – plush, figure and trading card box.

The series consisted of a plush toy in a bag, a pearly finish figure with PokéBall and a trading card game box containing two Generations boosters plus a promo card and pin badge, all featuring the legendary of the month. Each month featured a different retailer with the items being sold exclusively through them.

The Pokémon were as follows: February – Mew; March – Celebi; April – Jirachi; May – Darkrai; June – Manaphy*; July – Shaymin; August – Arceus; September – Victini; October – Keldeo; November – Genesect; December – Meloetta. *Unfortunately, there was one problem with Manaphy's distribution. Due to a stock problem at Tomy USA, the UK never saw the Manaphy plush hit stores at all, meaning importing was necessary in order to complete the full collection.

Although each was exclusive to a certain branch, later Pokémon, mainly Keldo, Genesect and Meloetta, were later given to discount stores. From their original £14.99 retail price they dropped to an incredible £1, where they were once again snapped up by savvy shoppers looking for a bargain on a franchise that doesn't see heavily discounted products often.

Chapter Nine
Alola

With *Pokémon Go* boosting the franchise to new heights, it was only natural that the next main games in the series – *Pokémon Sun* and *Moon* – would be huge hits for the franchise. This series included some major changes to the elements of the game, such as gyms no longer existing, replaced with challenges instead. The games were met with mixed responses, and the merchandise for Alolan characters in the UK was quickly shafted in favour of the classic characters featured prominently in *Pokémon Go* at the time.

Nintendo kickstarted the next installment with a special midnight release party. Tickets were handed out to those lucky enough to win them via various contests, and the event was held in London. Several promotional items were given away here, including a Rotom notebook (which includes a map of the Alola Region and artwork of the new starters), a Sun/Moon keychain, a Sun/Moon multi-pen, a PokéBall magnet and several different colouring sheets. A food voucher was given to every guest who attended, but most of these were handed in and thus there aren't many left in the wild. Shigeki Morimoto was also present at the event, and was happy to sign fans' items for free (with a limit of one per person, which, given the huge attendance, was very

Above left: Alola 'Rotom' PokéDex, Litten, Rowlett and Popplio Tomy plush.

Above right: *Pokémon Sun* and *Moon* event items – Rotom notebook, PokéBall coaster and multi-pen.

fair). Interestingly, Pokémon Center plush toys of the starters were on show and people could take photos of them and hold them, but they were not available for purchase.

Merchandise for *Sun* and *Moon* was pretty good overall, if a bit lacking in variety. The large legendary figures returned, as did the line of plush and figures.

With the debut of Alolan forms, the series took the time to reintroduce some collectors to the original Pokémon from Kanto, namely for those entering the franchise again from *Pokémon Go*. As such, some characters, such as Raichu, received merchandise of both their original forms and their Alolan forms. These two approximately 7–8 in. plushes were only seen in stores for a short time. Not because they were limited, but because they sold out too fast.

As mentioned before, the original Pokémon, particularly those from the Kanto region, featured heavily on Pokémon products. This entire wave consisted purely of other Pokémon and, despite being in a Sun/Moon box, has no Sun/Moon Pokémon available in this wave. Just beneath them, we can see some other figures from the Moncolle's UK line, from three individual series. Following the pattern started in Kalos, every series contains at least one Pikachu figure. This marketing strategy has received mixed opinions from fans, with some understanding the reason, and others who believe that the aggressive marketing towards Pikachu is unnecessary considering that other popular characters have yet to receive any figures in the UK. The latter opinion often extends to the entirety of Kanto, which is something else that was seen frequently in the Alola merchandise ranges.

An assortment of *Sun* and *Moon* merchandise. Other items, such as the Every Day Calendar shown here, popped up here and there. As can be seen in the figure collection, however, the original Kanto Pokémon were nearly as abundant as the Alolan Pokémon.

Raichu and Alolan
Raichu Tomy
plush.

Sun and *Moon* Tomy Moncolle figures (Bounsweet *v.* Pikachu, Salandit *v.* Pikachu and Popplio *v.* Pikachu).

But it's not all doom and gloom. New characters still appeared here and there, both in figure and plush form. In fact, after Wicked Cool Toys took over the line, there appears to be more new characters than before. Sure, we still have earlier region Pokémon popping up in some sets, but at least we finally received final evolution toys for this gen.

Chapter Ten
Ryme City

The year 2019 saw the release of the first ever live action Pokémon movie. This movie turned away from the usual training aspect seen in the majority of games and was instead based on a spin-off game known as *Detective Pikachu*. Fans were torn on what to think of the realistic appearance of the Pokémon, but the general response was positive. The collectibles made for the movie are unique compared to most other merchandise, though once again, the UK released very little outside of the trading cards and the movie received less than stellar advertising.

Unfortunately, much of the merchandise available for this movie was, in the UK at least, promotional. A figure set was released two months after the movie debuted in cinemas, as were a set of two-figure packs and a larger Detective Pikachu plush. A non-talking Pikachu plush was also released, but the talking version remains in

Detective Pikachu plush and promotional cube.

Promotional *Detective Pikachu* standee, cubes, display stand and oval standee. Perhaps not the easiest items to get hold of unless you know who to ask. Standees and display units such as these make excellent focal points for a collection. Unfortunately, they are becoming increasingly more difficult to obtain, since companies do not appreciate their kindness being taken advantage of when these appear on auction sites. It's always worth asking!

the US, where it is strangely priced the same as the non-talking plush. Promotional items, such as the two caps and bracelets seen here, were given as prizes to contest winners or to popular social media channel owners for them to generate hype. A *Detective Pikachu* pop-up event was held in London, although merchandise was not purchasable. That being said, people who attended received cardboard ears, a cup and a bottle.

Chapter Eleven
Galar

The future is Galar, the region inspired by the UK which will mark a new journey for Pokémon trainers around the world. With starters Sobble, Scorbunny and Grookey and Dynamaxing at their disposal, it's sure to be another hit for the franchise as a whole. What new merchandise awaits us is unknown, but that's always the fun of a new generation of Pokémon. Pre-order gifts have already been added for several countries, including the UK, where we can receive a figure of the new starter trio with the purchase of the dual steel book editions of *Sword* and *Shield*. Whilst only a pop-up that will have closed by the time this book has been released, Pokémon Center London was finally made a reality. Perhaps in the future it will see a permanent return.

It's probably wishful thinking, but who knows what's around the corner. All we know is the series' immortal words – Gotta catch 'em all.